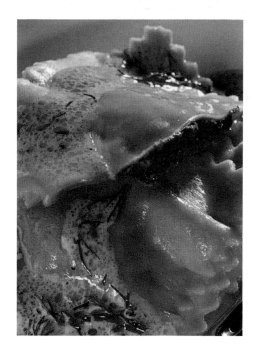

Starters & Light Meals

If you are looking for something tasty and simple to make, or the perfect pasta starter for a meal, then take a look at this delicious range of recipe ideas.

Main Courses

Pasta makes a fantastic main course, with plenty of different shapes and sizes to choose from. It makes a healthy, wholesome meal for friends and family.

FLAME TREE has been creating family-friendly, classic and beginner recipes for our bestselling cookbooks for over 12 years now. Our mission is to offer you a wide range of expert-tested dishes, while providing clear images of the final dish so that you can match it to your own results. We hope you enjoy this super selection of recipes – there are plenty more to try! Titles in this series include:

**Cupcakes • Slow Cooker • Curries
Chinese • Soups • Baking Breads
Cakes • Simple Suppers • Pasta
Chicken • Fish & Seafood • Chocolate**

For more information please visit:
www.flametreepublishing.com

Louisiana Prawns & Fettuccine

INGREDIENTS

Serves 4

4 tbsp olive oil

450 g/1 lb raw tiger prawns, washed
   and peeled, shells and
   heads reserved

2 shallots, peeled and finely chopped

4 garlic cloves, peeled and
   finely chopped

large handful fresh basil leaves

1 carrot, peeled and finely chopped

1 onion, peeled and finely chopped

1 celery stick, trimmed and
   finely chopped

2–3 sprigs fresh parsley

2–3 sprigs fresh thyme

salt and freshly ground black pepper

pinch cayenne pepper

175 ml/6 fl oz dry white wine

450 g/1 lb ripe tomatoes,
   roughly chopped

juice of ½ lemon, or to taste

350 g/12 oz fettuccine

1 Heat 2 tablespoons of the olive oil in a large saucepan and add the reserved prawn shells and heads. Fry over a high heat for 2–3 minutes, until the shells turn pink and are lightly browned. Add half the shallots, half the garlic, half the basil and the carrot, onion, celery, parsley and thyme. Season lightly with salt, pepper and cayenne and sauté for 2–3 minutes, stirring often.

2 Pour in the wine and stir, scraping the pan well. Bring to the boil and simmer for 1 minute, then add the tomatoes. Cook for a further 3–4 minutes then pour in 200 ml/7 fl oz water. Bring to the boil, lower the heat and simmer for about 30 minutes, stirring often and using a wooden spoon to mash the prawn shells in order to release as much flavour as possible into the sauce. Lower the heat if the sauce is reducing very quickly.

3 Strain through a sieve, pressing well to extract as much liquid as possible; there should be about 450 ml/¾ pint. Pour the liquid into a clean pan and bring to the boil, then lower the heat and simmer gently until the liquid is reduced by about half.

4 Heat the remaining olive oil over a high heat in a clean frying pan and add the peeled prawns. Season lightly and add the lemon juice. Cook for 1 minute, lower the heat and add the remaining shallots and garlic. Cook for 1 minute. Add the sauce and adjust the seasoning.

5 Meanwhile, bring a large pan of lightly salted water to a rolling boil and add the fettuccine. Cook according to the packet instructions, or until 'al dente', and drain thoroughly. Transfer to a warmed serving dish. Add the sauce and toss well. Garnish with the remaining basil and serve immediately.

Pasta with Walnut Sauce

INGREDIENTS

Serves 4

50 g/2 oz walnuts, toasted
3 spring onions, trimmed
   and chopped
2 garlic cloves, peeled and sliced
1 tbsp freshly chopped parsley
   or basil
5 tbsp extra virgin olive oil
salt and freshly ground black pepper
450 g/1 lb broccoli, cut into florets
350 g/12 oz pasta shapes
1 red chilli, deseeded and
   finely chopped

HELPFUL HINT

There is no hard-and-fast rule about which shape of pasta to use with this recipe; it is really a matter of personal preference. Spirali have been used here, but rigatoni, farfalle, garganelle or pipe rigate would all work well, or you could choose flavoured pasta, such as tomato, or a wholewheat variety for a change.

1 Place the toasted walnuts in a blender or food processor with the chopped spring onions, one of the garlic cloves and parsley or basil. Blend to a fairly smooth paste, then gradually add 3 tablespoons of the olive oil, until it is well mixed into the paste. Season the walnut paste to taste with salt and pepper and reserve.

2 Bring a large pan of lightly salted water to a rolling boil. Add the broccoli, return to the boil and cook for 2 minutes. Remove the broccoli, using a slotted draining spoon and refresh under cold running water. Drain again and pat dry on absorbent kitchen paper.

3 Bring the water back to a rolling boil. Add the pasta and cook according to the packet instructions, or until 'al dente'.

4 Meanwhile, heat the remaining oil in a frying pan. Add the remaining garlic and chilli. Cook gently for 2 minutes, or until softened. Add the broccoli and walnut paste. Cook for a further 3–4 minutes, or until heated through.

5 Drain the pasta thoroughly and transfer to a large warmed serving bowl. Pour over the walnut and broccoli sauce. Toss together, adjust the seasoning and serve immediately.

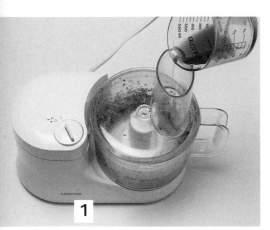

Beetroot Ravioli with Dill Cream Sauce

INGREDIENTS

Serves 4–6

fresh pasta dough (see p48)

1 tbsp olive oil

1 small onion, peeled and finely chopped

½ tsp caraway seeds

175 g/6 oz cooked beetroot, chopped

175 g/6 oz ricotta cheese

25 g/1 oz fresh white breadcrumbs

1 medium egg yolk

2 tbsp grated Parmesan cheese

salt and freshly ground black pepper

4 tbsp walnut oil

4 tbsp freshly chopped dill

1 tbsp green peppercorns, drained and roughly chopped

6 tbsp crème fraîche

1. Make the pasta dough (see p48). Wrap in clingfilm and leave to rest for 30 minutes.

2. Heat the olive oil in a large frying pan, add the onion and caraway seeds and cook over a medium heat for 5 minutes, or until the onion is softened and lightly golden. Stir in the beetroot and cook for 5 minutes.

3. Blend the beetroot mixture in a food processor until smooth, then allow to cool. Stir in the ricotta cheese, breadcrumbs, egg yolk and Parmesan cheese. Season to taste with salt and pepper, and reserve.

4. Divide the pasta dough into 8 pieces. Roll out as for tagliatelle, but do not cut the sheets in half. Lay 1 sheet on a floured surface and place 5 heaped teaspoons of the filling 2.5 cm/1 inch apart.

5. Dampen around the heaps of filling and lay a second sheet of pasta over the top. Press around the heaps to seal. Cut into squares using a pastry wheel or sharp knife. Put the filled pasta shapes on to a floured tea towel.

6. Bring a large pan of lightly salted water to a rolling boil. Drop the ravioli into the boiling water, return to the boil and cook for 3–4 minutes, until 'al dente'.

7. Meanwhile, heat the walnut oil in a small pan then add the chopped dill and green peppercorns. Remove from the heat, stir in the crème fraîche and season well. Drain the cooked pasta thoroughly and toss with the sauce. Tip into warmed serving dishes and serve immediately.

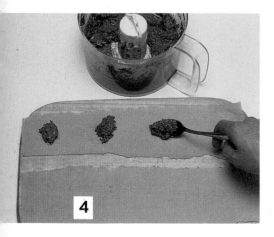

4

5

5

Spinach & Ricotta Gnocchi with Butter & Parmesan

INGREDIENTS

Serves 2–4

125 g/4 oz frozen leaf
   spinach, thawed
225 g/8 oz ricotta cheese
2 small eggs, lightly beaten
50 g/2 oz freshly grated
   Parmesan cheese
salt and freshly ground black pepper
2 tbsp freshly chopped basil
50 g/2 oz plain flour
50 g/2 oz unsalted butter
2 garlic cloves, peeled and crushed
Parmesan cheese shavings, to serve

FOOD FACT

Ricotta is a crumbly, soft white cheese made from ewes' milk whey, a by-product from the manufacture of Pecorino Romano cheese. The curd is compacted so that the cheese can be cut with a knife. It can be eaten by itself, but normally it is used in dishes such as cheesecake.

1 Squeeze the excess moisture from the spinach and chop finely. Blend in a food processor with the ricotta cheese, eggs, Parmesan cheese, seasoning and 1 tablespoon of the basil until smooth. Scrape into a bowl then add sufficient flour to form a soft, slightly sticky dough.

2 Bring a large pan of salted water to a rolling boil. Transfer the spinach mixture to a piping bag fitted with a large plain nozzle. As soon as the water is boiling, pipe 10–12 short lengths of the mixture into the water, using a sharp knife to cut the gnocchi as you go.

3 Bring the water back to the boil and cook the gnocchi for 3–4 minutes, or until they begin to rise to the surface. Remove with a slotted spoon, drain on absorbent kitchen paper and transfer to a warmed serving dish. Cook the gnocchi in batches if necessary.

4 Melt the butter in a small frying pan and when foaming add the garlic and remaining basil. Remove from the heat and immediately pour over the cooked gnocchi. Season well with salt and pepper and serve immediately with extra grated Parmesan cheese.

Spaghetti with Fresh Tomatoes, Chilli & Potatoes

INGREDIENTS

Serves 6

2 medium potatoes, unpeeled

3 garlic cloves, peeled and crushed

1 small bunch basil, roughly chopped

6 tbsp olive oil

4 large ripe plum tomatoes, skinned, seeded and chopped

1 small red chilli, deseeded and finely chopped

salt and freshly ground black pepper

450 g/1 lb spaghetti

4 tbsp freshly grated Parmesan cheese, to serve (optional)

1 Preheat the grill to high 5 minutes before using. Cook the potatoes in plenty of boiling water until tender but firm. Allow to cool, then peel and cut into cubes.

2 Blend the garlic, basil and 4 tablespoons of the olive oil in a blender or food processor until the basil is finely chopped, then reserve.

3 Place the tomatoes, basil and oil mixture in a small bowl, add the chilli and season with salt and pepper to taste. Mix together and reserve the sauce.

4 Bring a large pan of salted water to a rolling boil, add the spaghetti and cook according to the packet instructions, or until 'al dente'.

5 Meanwhile, toss the potato cubes with the remaining olive oil and transfer to a baking sheet. Place the potatoes under the preheated grill until they are crisp and golden, turning once or twice, then drain on absorbent kitchen paper.

6 Drain the pasta thoroughly and transfer to a warmed shallow serving bowl. Add the tomato sauce and the hot potatoes. Toss well and adjust the seasoning to taste. Serve immediately with the grated Parmesan cheese, if using.

2

3

5

Pasta Genovese with Pesto, Green Beans & Potatoes

INGREDIENTS

Serves 6

40 g/1½ oz basil leaves

2 garlic cloves, peeled and crushed

2 tbsp pine nuts, lightly toasted

25 g/1 oz freshly grated
   Parmesan cheese

75 ml/3 fl oz extra virgin olive oil

salt and freshly ground pepper

175 g/6 oz new potatoes, scrubbed

125 g/4 oz fine French
   beans, trimmed

2 tbsp olive oil

450 g/1 lb pasta shapes

extra freshly grated Parmesan
   cheese, to serve

TASTY TIP

Classic pesto is made with fresh basil and pine nuts, but other herb variations work equally well. Try replacing the basil with fresh coriander leaves and adding a deseeded and finely chopped red chilli, or try an almond and mint pesto, using blanched almonds, mint and fresh parsley.

1 Put the basil leaves, garlic, pine nuts and Parmesan cheese into a food processor and blend until finely chopped. Transfer the mixture in to a small bowl and stir in the olive oil. Season the pesto to taste with salt and pepper and reserve.

2 Bring a pan of salted water to boil and cook the potatoes for 12–14 minutes, or until tender. About 4 minutes before the end of the cooking time, add the beans. Drain well and refresh under cold water. Reserve the beans and slice the potatoes thickly, or halve them if small.

3 Heat the olive oil in a frying pan and add the potatoes. Fry over a medium heat for 5 minutes, or until golden. Add the reserved beans and pesto and cook for a further 2 minutes.

4 Meanwhile, bring a large pan of lightly salted water to a rolling boil. Cook the pasta shapes according to the packet instructions, or until 'al dente'. Drain thoroughly, return to the pan and add the pesto mixture. Toss well and heat through for 1–2 minutes. Tip into a warmed serving bowl and serve immediately with Parmesan cheese.

1

3

4

Tiny Pasta with Fresh Herb Sauce

INGREDIENTS

Serves 6

375 g/13 oz tripolini (small bows with
   rounded ends) or small farfalle
2 tbsp freshly chopped flat
   leaf parsley
2 tbsp freshly chopped basil
1 tbsp freshly snipped chives
1 tbsp freshly chopped chervil
1 tbsp freshly chopped tarragon
1 tbsp freshly chopped sage
1 tbsp freshly chopped oregano
1 tbsp freshly chopped marjoram
1 tbsp freshly chopped thyme
1 tbsp freshly chopped rosemary
finely grated zest of 1 lemon
75 ml/3 fl oz extra virgin olive oil
2 garlic cloves, peeled and
   finely chopped
½ tsp dried chilli flakes
salt and freshly ground black pepper
freshly grated Parmesan cheese,
   to serve

1 Bring a large pan of lightly salted water to a rolling boil. Add the pasta and cook according to the packet instructions, or until 'al dente'.

2 Meanwhile, place all the herbs, the lemon zest, olive oil, garlic and chilli flakes in a heavy-based pan. Heat gently for 2–3 minutes, or until the herbs turn bright green and become very fragrant. Remove from the heat and season to taste with salt and pepper.

3 Drain the pasta thoroughly, reserving 2–3 tablespoons of the cooking water. Transfer the pasta to a large warmed bowl.

4 Pour the heated herb mixture over the pasta and toss together until thoroughly mixed. Check and adjust the seasoning, adding a little of the pasta cooking water if the pasta mixture seems a bit dry. Transfer to warmed serving dishes and serve immediately with grated Parmesan cheese.

2

3

4

Spaghettini with Peas, Spring Onions & Mint

INGREDIENTS

Serves 6

pinch saffron strands

700 g/1½ lb fresh peas or

  350 g/12 oz frozen petit pois, thawed

75 g/3 oz unsalted butter, softened

6 spring onions, trimmed and

  finely sliced

salt and freshly ground black pepper

1 garlic clove, peeled and

  finely chopped

2 tbsp freshly chopped mint

1 tbsp freshly snipped chives

450 g/1 lb spaghettini

freshly grated Parmesan cheese,

  to serve

HELPFUL HINT

To develop the full flavour and deep golden colour of the saffron, it should be soaked for at least 20 minutes, so do this well before you start cooking. Saffron is one of the few spices that can be kept for several years, but you must store it in an airtight container, away from light.

1 Soak the saffron in 2 tablespoons hot water while you prepare the sauce. Shell the peas if using fresh ones.

2 Heat 50 g/2 oz of the butter in a medium frying pan, add the spring onions and a little salt and cook over a low heat for 2–3 minutes, or until the onions are softened. Add the garlic, then the peas and 100 ml/3½ fl oz water. Bring to the boil and cook for 5–6 minutes, or until the peas are just tender. Stir in the mint and keep warm.

3 Blend the remaining butter and the saffron water in a large warmed serving bowl and reserve.

4 Meanwhile, bring a large pan of lightly salted water to a rolling boil and add the spaghettini. Cook according to the packet instructions, or until 'al dente'.

5 Drain thoroughly, reserving 2–3 tablespoons of the pasta cooking water. Tip into a warmed serving bowl, add the pea sauce and toss together gently. Season to taste with salt and pepper. Serve immediately with extra black pepper and grated Parmesan cheese.

2

3

5

Fusilli with Spicy Tomato & Chorizo Sauce with Roasted Peppers

INGREDIENTS

Serves 6

4 tbsp olive oil

1 red pepper, deseeded and quartered

1 yellow pepper, deseeded
  and quartered

175 g/6 oz chorizo (outer skin
  removed), roughly chopped

2 garlic cloves, peeled and finely
  chopped

large pinch chilli flakes

700 g/1½ lb ripe tomatoes, skinned
  and roughly chopped

salt and freshly ground black pepper

450 g/1 lb fusilli

basil leaves, to garnish

freshly grated Parmesan cheese,
  to serve

FOOD FACT

There are two types of chorizo: dried, usually about 5 cm/2 in in diameter, and the slightly softer, semi-dried chorizo, which look like short fat sausages. The latter is used here. Both types contain chilli and paprika, hence their colour.

1 Preheat the grill to high. Brush the pepper quarters with 1 tablespoon of the olive oil, then cook under the preheated grill, turning once, for 8–10 minutes, or until the skins have blackened and the flesh is tender. Place the peppers in a plastic bag until cool enough to handle. When cooled, peel the peppers, slice very thinly and reserve.

2 Heat the remaining oil in a frying pan and add the chorizo. Cook over a medium heat for 3–4 minutes, or until starting to brown. Add the garlic and chilli flakes and cook for a further 2–3 minutes.

3 Add the tomatoes, season lightly with salt and pepper then cook gently for about 5 minutes, or until the tomatoes have broken down. Lower the heat and cook for a further 10–15 minutes, or until the sauce has thickened. Add the peppers and heat gently for 1-2 minutes. Adjust the seasoning to taste.

4 Meanwhile, bring a large pan of lightly salted water to a rolling boil. Add the fusilli and cook according to the packet instructions, or until 'al dente'. Drain thoroughly and transfer to a warmed serving dish. Pour over the sauce, sprinkle with basil and serve with Parmesan cheese.

1

2

3

Gnocchetti with Broccoli & Bacon Sauce

INGREDIENTS

Serves 6

450 g/1 lb broccoli florets

4 tbsp olive oil

50 g/2 oz pancetta or smoked
  bacon, finely chopped

1 small onion, peeled and
  finely chopped

3 garlic cloves, peeled and sliced

200 ml/7 fl oz milk

450 g/1 lb gnocchetti (little elongated
  ribbed shells)

50 g/2 oz freshly grated Parmesan
  cheese, plus extra to serve

salt and freshly ground black pepper

FOOD FACT

Pancetta is an Italian streaky bacon that may be either smoked or unsmoked. You can buy it sliced or in a piece, but it is often sold pre-packed, cut into tiny cubes ready for cooking. Thickly cut, rindless smoked streaky bacon makes a good alternative.

1 Bring a large pan of salted water to the boil. Add the broccoli florets and cook for about 8–10 minutes, or until very soft. Drain thoroughly, allow to cool slightly then chop finely and reserve.

2 Heat the olive oil in a heavy-based pan, add the pancetta or bacon and cook over a medium heat for 5 minutes, or until golden and crisp. Add the onion and cook for a further 5 minutes, or until soft and lightly golden. Add the garlic and cook for 1 minute.

3 Transfer the chopped broccoli to the bacon or pancetta mixture and pour in the milk. Bring slowly to the boil and simmer rapidly for about 15 minutes, or until reduced to a creamy texture.

4 Meanwhile, bring a large pan of lightly salted water to a rolling boil. Add the pasta and cook according to the packet instructions, or until 'al dente'.

5 Drain the pasta thoroughly, reserving a little of the cooking water. Add the pasta and the Parmesan cheese to the broccoli mixture. Toss, adding enough of the reserved cooking water to make a creamy sauce. Season to taste with salt and pepper. Serve immediately with extra Parmesan cheese.

Penne with Artichokes, Bacon & Mushrooms

INGREDIENTS

Serves 6

2 tbsp olive oil

75 g/3 oz smoked bacon or
   pancetta, chopped

1 small onion, peeled and finely sliced

125 g/4 oz chestnut mushrooms,
   wiped and sliced

2 garlic cloves, peeled and
   finely chopped

400 g/14 oz can artichoke hearts,
   drained and halved or quartered
   if large

100 ml/3½ fl oz dry white wine

100 ml/3½ fl oz chicken stock

3 tbsp double cream

50 g/2 oz freshly grated Parmesan
   cheese, plus extra to serve

salt and freshly ground black pepper

450 g/1 lb penne

shredded basil leaves, to garnish

TASTY TIP

Chestnut mushrooms are orange-brown in colour and have a nutty flavour. Baby chestnut mushrooms could also be used in this recipe.

1 Heat the olive oil in a frying pan and add the pancetta or bacon and the onion. Cook over a medium heat for 8–10 minutes, or until the bacon is crisp and the onion is just golden. Add the mushrooms and garlic and cook for a further 5 minutes, or until softened.

2 Add the artichoke hearts to the mushroom mixture and cook for 3–4 minutes. Pour in the wine, bring to the boil then simmer rapidly until the liquid is reduced and syrupy.

3 Pour in the chicken stock, bring to the boil then simmer rapidly for about 5 minutes, or until slightly reduced. Reduce the heat slightly, then slowly stir in the double cream and Parmesan cheese. Season the sauce to taste with salt and pepper.

4 Meanwhile, bring a large pan of lightly salted water to a rolling boil. Add the pasta and cook according to the packet instructions, or until 'al dente'.

5 Drain the pasta thoroughly and transfer to a large warmed serving dish. Pour over the sauce and toss together. Garnish with shredded basil and serve with extra Parmesan cheese.

1

2

3

Fettuccine with Wild Mushrooms & Prosciutto

INGREDIENTS

Serves 6

15 g/½ oz dried porcini mushrooms
150 ml/¼ pint hot chicken stock
2 tbsp olive oil
1 small onion, peeled and
    finely chopped
2 garlic cloves, peeled and
    finely chopped
4 slices prosciutto, chopped or torn
225 g/8 oz mixed wild or cultivated
    mushrooms, wiped and sliced
    if necessary
450 g/1 lb fettuccine
3 tbsp crème fraîche
2 tbsp freshly chopped parsley
salt and freshly ground black pepper
freshly grated Parmesan cheese,
    to serve (optional)

FOOD FACT

Prosciutto is produced from pigs fed on Parmesan whey. The ham is dry cured, weighted to flatten it and give it a dense texture, and left to mature. It is often served raw in paper-thin slices.

1. Place the dried mushrooms in a small bowl and pour over the hot chicken stock. Leave to soak for 15–20 minutes, or until the mushrooms have softened.

2. Meanwhile, heat the olive oil in a large frying pan. Add the onion and cook for 5 minutes over a medium heat, or until softened. Add the garlic and cook for 1 minute, then add the prosciutto and cook for a further minute.

3. Drain the dried mushrooms, reserving the soaking liquid. Roughly chop and add to the frying pan together with the fresh mushrooms. Cook over a high heat for 5 minutes, stirring often, or until softened. Strain the mushroom soaking liquid into the pan.

4. Meanwhile, bring a large pan of lightly salted water to a rolling boil. Add the pasta and cook according to the packet instructions, or until 'al dente'.

5. Stir the crème fraîche and chopped parsley into the mushroom mixture and heat through gently. Season to taste with salt and pepper. Drain the pasta well, transfer to a large warmed serving dish and pour over the sauce. Serve immediately with grated Parmesan cheese.

Spaghetti Bolognese

INGREDIENTS

SERVES 4

3 tbsp olive oil

50 g/2 oz unsmoked streaky bacon,
  rind removed and chopped

1 small onion, peeled and
  finely chopped

1 carrot, peeled and finely chopped

1 celery, trimmed and finely chopped

2 garlic cloves, peeled and crushed

1 bay leaf

500 g/1 lb 2 oz minced beef steak

400 g can chopped tomatoes

2 tbsp tomato paste

150 ml/ ¼ pint red wine

150 ml/ ¼ pint beef stock

salt and freshly ground black pepper

450 g/1 lb spaghetti

freshly grated Parmesan cheese,
  to serve

FOOD FACT

Ragù alla Bolognese, as it is known in Italy, is enjoyed all over the world, especially in the United States and Britain. It originated in the city of Bologna in Emilia-Romagna, where it is served with tagliatelle, rather than spaghetti.

1 Heat the olive oil in a large heavy-based pan, add the bacon and cook for 5 minutes or until slightly coloured. Add the onion, carrot, celery, garlic and bay leaf and cook, stirring, for 8 minutes, or until the vegetables are soft.

2 Add the minced beef to the pan and cook, stirring with a wooden spoon to break up any lumps in the meat, for 5-8 minutes, or until browned.

3 Stir the tomatoes and tomato paste into the mince and pour in the wine and stock. Bring to the boil, lower the heat and simmer for a least 40 minutes, stirring occasionally. The longer you leave the sauce to cook, the more intense the flavour. Season to taste with salt and pepper and remove the bay leaf.

4 Meanwhile, bring a large pan of lightly salted water to a rolling boil, add the spaghetti and cook for about 8 minutes or until 'al dente'. Drain and arrange on warmed serving plates. Top with the prepared Bolognese sauce and serve immediately sprinkled with grated Parmesan cheese.

Lasagne

INGREDIENTS

SERVES 4

75 g/3 oz butter
4 tbsp plain flour
750 ml/ ¼ pint milk
1 tsp wholegrain mustard
salt and freshly ground black pepper
¼ tsp freshly grated nutmeg
9 sheets lasagne
1 quantity of prepared Bolognese
    sauce (see p26)
75 g/3 oz freshly grated
    Parmesan cheese
freshly chopped parsley, to garnish
garlic bread, to serve

HELPFUL HINT

For a change use lasagne verdi – it is green lasagne made with spinach. The shape varies according to the manufacturer and may be flat or wavy. Some have crimped edges, which help to trap the sauce and stop it running to the bottom of the dish. As brands come in slightly different sizes, it is worth trying several until you find the one that fits your lasagne dish perfectly!

1   Preheat the oven to 200°C/400°F/Gas Mark 6, 15 minutes before cooking. Melt the butter in a small heavy-based pan, add the flour and cook gently, stirring, for 2 minutes. Remove from the heat and gradually stir in the milk. Return to the heat and cook, stirring, for 2 minutes, or until the sauce thickens. Bring to the boil, remove from the heat and stir in the mustard. Season to taste with salt, pepper and nutmeg.

2   Butter a rectangular ovenproof dish and spread a thin layer of the white sauce over the base. Cover completely with 3 sheets of lasagne.

3   Spoon a quarter of the prepared Bolognese sauce over the lasagne. Spoon over a quarter of the remaining white sauce, then sprinkle with a quarter of the grated Parmesan cheese. Repeat the layers, finishing with Parmesan cheese.

4   Bake in the preheated oven for 30 minutes, or until golden-brown. Garnish with chopped parsley and serve immediately with warm garlic bread.

1

2

3

Spicy Chilli Beef with Fusili

INGREDIENTS

Serves 4

2 tbsp olive oil

1 onion, peeled and finely chopped

1 red pepper, deseeded and sliced

450 g/1 lb minced beef steak

2 garlic cloves, peeled and crushed

2 red chillies, deseeded and finely
   sliced

salt and freshly ground black pepper

400 g can chopped tomatoes

2 tbsp tomato paste

400 g can red kidney beans, drained

50 g/2 oz good quality, plain dark
   chocolate, grated

350 g/12 oz dried fusilli

knob of butter

2 tbsp freshly chopped flat-leaf parsley

paprika, to garnish

soured cream, to serve

FOOD FACT

Chocolate in sauces adds rich warm undertones, colour and slight sweetness, but no-one will realise it is there unless you tell them. Use a good quality, plain dark chocolate with a minimum sugar content and a high percentage of cocoa solids.

1 Heat the olive oil in a large heavy-based pan. Add the onion and red pepper and cook for 5 minutes, or until beginning to soften. Add the minced beef and cook over a high heat for 5–8 minutes, or until the meat is browned. Stir with a wooden spoon during cooking to break up any lumps in the meat. Add the garlic and chilli, fry for 1 minute then season to taste with salt and pepper.

2 Add the chopped tomatoes, tomato paste and the kidney beans to the pan. Bring to the boil, lower the heat, and simmer, covered, for at least 40 minutes, stirring occasionally. Stir in the grated chocolate and cook for 3 minutes, or until melted.

3 Meanwhile, bring a large pan of lightly salted water to a rolling boil. Add the fusilli and cook according to the packet instructions, or until 'al dente'.

4 Drain the pasta, return to the pan and toss with the butter and parsley. Tip into a warmed serving dish or spoon on to individual plates. Spoon the sauce over the pasta. Sprinkle with paprika and serve immediately with spoonfuls of soured cream.

Gnocchi & Parma Ham Bake

INGREDIENTS

Serves 4

3 tbsp olive oil

1 red onion, peeled and sliced

2 garlic cloves, peeled

175 g/6 oz plum tomatoes, skinned
  and quartered

2 tbsp sun-dried tomato paste

250 g tub mascarpone cheese

salt and freshly ground black pepper

1 tbsp freshly chopped tarragon

300 g/11 oz fresh gnocchi

125 g/4 oz Cheddar or Parmesan
  cheese, grated

50 g/2 oz fresh white breadcrumbs

50 g/2 oz Parma ham, sliced

10 pitted green olives, halved

sprigs of flat leaf parsley, to garnish

HELPFUL HINT

Make sure that you buy gnocchi potato dumplings for this recipe and not gnocchi sardi, a pasta of the same name. It is important to use a large pan so that the gnocchi have room to move around, as they can stick together during cooking. If necessary, cook the gnocchi in two batches.

1 Heat the oven to 180°C/350°F/Gas Mark 4, 10 minutes before cooking. Heat 2 tablespoons of the olive oil in a large frying pan and cook the onion and garlic for 5 minutes, or until softened. Stir in the tomatoes, sun-dried tomato paste and mascarpone cheese. Season to taste with salt and pepper. Add half the tarragon. Bring to the boil, then lower the heat immediately and simmer for 5 minutes.

2 Meanwhile, bring 1.7 litres/3 pints water to the boil in a large pan. Add the remaining olive oil and a good pinch of salt. Add the gnocchi and cook for 1–2 minutes, or until they rise to the surface.

3 Drain the gnocchi thoroughly and transfer to a large ovenproof dish. Add the tomato sauce and toss gently to coat the pasta. Combine the Cheddar or Parmesan cheese with the breadcrumbs and remaining tarragon and scatter over the pasta mixture. Top with the Parma ham and olives and season again.

4 Cook in the preheated oven for 20–25 minutes, or until golden and bubbling. Serve immediately, garnished with parsley sprigs.

Lamb Arrabbiata

INGREDIENTS

Serves 4

4 tbsp olive oil

450 g/1 lb lamb fillets, cubed

1 large onion, peeled and sliced

4 garlic cloves, peeled and
 finely chopped

1 red chilli, deseeded and
 finely chopped

400 g can chopped tomatoes

175 g/6 oz pitted black olives, halved

150 ml/ ¼ pint white wine

salt and freshly ground black pepper

275 g/10 oz farfalle pasta

1 tsp butter

4 tbsp freshly chopped parsley, plus
 1 tbsp to garnish

HELPFUL HINT

When cooking pasta, remember to use a very large saucepan so that the pasta has plenty of room to move around freely. Once the water has come to the boil, add the pasta, stir, cover with a lid and return to the boil. The lid can then be removed so that the water does not boil over.

1 Heat 2 tablespoons of the olive oil in a large frying pan and cook the lamb for 5–7 minutes, or until sealed. Remove from the pan using a slotted spoon and reserve.

2 Heat the remaining oil in the pan, add the onion, garlic and chilli and cook until softened. Add the tomatoes, bring to the boil, then simmer for 10 minutes.

3 Return the browned lamb to the pan with the olives and pour in the wine. Bring the sauce back to the boil, reduce the heat then simmer, uncovered, for 15 minutes, until the lamb is tender. Season to taste with salt and pepper.

4 Meanwhile, bring a large pan of lightly salted water to a rolling boil. Add the pasta and cook according to the packet instructions, or until 'al dente'.

5 Drain the pasta, toss in the butter, then add to the sauce and mix lightly. Stir in 4 tablespoons of the chopped parsley, then tip into a warmed serving dish. Sprinkle with the remaining parsley and serve immediately.

2

3

5

Creamy Turkey & Tomato Pasta

INGREDIENTS

Serves 4

4 tbsp olive oil

450 g/1 lb turkey breasts, cut into
  bite-sized pieces

550 g/1¼ lb cherry tomatoes,
  on the vine

2 garlic cloves, peeled and chopped

4 tbsp balsamic vinegar

4 tbsp freshly chopped basil

salt and freshly ground black pepper

200 ml tub crème fraîche

350 g/12 oz tagliatelle

shaved Parmesan cheese, to garnish

FOOD FACT

Balsamic vinegar is dark in colour with a mellow sweet and sour flavour. It is made from concentrated grape juice and fermented in wooden barrels. Like good wine, the vinegar improves and becomes darker and more syrupy the longer it is aged. Less expensive vinegars bought from supermarkets have been matured for three or four years only. The flavour is nonetheless wonderful and perfect for this recipe.

1 Preheat the oven to 200°C/400°F/Gas Mark 6. Heat 2 tablespoons of the olive oil in a large frying pan. Add the turkey and cook for 5 minutes, or until sealed, turning occasionally. Transfer to a roasting tin and add the remaining olive oil, the vine tomatoes, garlic and balsamic vinegar. Stir well and season to taste with salt and pepper. Cook in the preheated oven for 30 minutes, or until the turkey is tender, turning the tomatoes and turkey once.

2 Meanwhile, bring a large pan of lightly salted water to a rolling boil. Add the pasta and cook according to the packet instructions, or until 'al dente'. Drain, return to the pan and keep warm. Stir the basil and seasoning into the crème fraîche.

3 Remove the roasting tin from the oven and discard the vines. Stir the crème fraîche and basil mix into the turkey and tomato mixture and return to the oven for 1–2 minutes, or until thoroughly heated through.

4 Stir the turkey and tomato mixture into the pasta and toss lightly together. Tip into a warmed serving dish. Garnish with Parmesan cheese shavings and serve immediately.

Cheesy Baked Chicken Macaroni

INGREDIENTS

Serves 4

1 tbsp olive oil

350 g/12 oz boneless and skinless
   chicken breasts, diced

75 g/3 oz pancetta, diced

1 onion, peeled and chopped

1 garlic clove, peeled and chopped

350 g packet fresh tomato sauce

400 g can chopped tomatoes

2 tbsp freshly chopped basil, plus
   leaves to garnish

salt and freshly ground black pepper

350 g/12 oz macaroni

150 g/5oz mozzarella cheese, drained
   and chopped

50 g/2 oz Gruyère cheese, grated

50 g/2 oz freshly grated
   Parmesan cheese

FOOD FACT

Pancetta (cured dried belly of pork) imparts a wonderful flavour to a dish; it is available from delicatessens and supermarkets.

1 Preheat the grill just before cooking. Heat the oil in large frying pan and cook the chicken for 8 minutes, or until browned, stirring occasionally. Drain on absorbent kitchen paper and reserve. Add the pancetta slices to the pan and fry on both sides until crispy. Remove from the pan and reserve.

2 Add the onion and garlic to the frying pan and cook for 5 minutes, or until softened. Stir in the tomato sauce, chopped tomatoes and basil and season to taste with salt and pepper. Bring to the boil, lower the heat and simmer the sauce for 5 minutes.

3 Meanwhile, bring a large pan of lightly salted water to a rolling boil. Add the macaroni and cook according to the packet instructions, or until 'al dente'.

4 Drain the macaroni thoroughly, return to the pan and stir in the sauce, chicken and mozzarella cheese. Spoon into a shallow ovenproof dish.

5 Sprinkle the pancetta over the macaroni. Sprinkle over the Gruyère and Parmesan cheeses. Place under the preheated grill and cook for 5–10 minutes, or until golden-brown; turn the dish occasionally. Garnish and serve immediately.

2

4

5

Penne with Pan-fried Chicken & Capers

INGREDIENTS

Serves 4

4 boneless and skinless
  chicken breasts
25 g/1 oz plain flour
salt and freshly ground black pepper
350 g/12 oz penne
2 tbsp olive oil
25 g/1 oz butter
1 red onion, peeled and sliced
1 garlic clove, peeled and chopped
4–6 tbsp pesto
250 g carton mascarpone cheese
1 tsp wholegrain mustard
1 tbsp lemon juice
2 tbsp freshly chopped basil
3 tbsp capers in brine, rinsed
  and drained
freshly shaved Pecorino
  Romano cheese

FOOD FACT

Pecorino Romano is a cooked, pressed cheese. It has a dense texture, pale yellow colour and almost smoky aroma. Its flavour is very salty, so take care when seasoning.

1 Trim the chicken and cut into bite-sized pieces. Season the flour with salt and pepper then toss the chicken in the seasoned flour and reserve.

2 Bring a large saucepan of lightly salted water to a rolling boil. Add the penne and cook according to the packet instructions, or until 'al dente'.

3 Meanwhile, heat the olive oil in a large frying pan. Add the chicken to the pan and cook for 8 minutes, or until golden on all sides, stirring frequently. Transfer the chicken to a plate and reserve.

4 Add the onion and garlic to the oil remaining in the frying pan and cook for 5 minutes, or until softened, stirring frequently.

5 Return the chicken to the frying pan. Stir in the pesto and mascarpone cheese and heat through, stirring gently, until smooth. Stir in the wholegrain mustard, lemon juice, basil and capers. Season to taste, then continue to heat through until piping hot.

6 Drain the penne thoroughly and return to the saucepan. Pour over the sauce and toss well to coat. Arrange the pasta on individual warmed plates. Scatter with the cheese and serve immediately.

Rigatoni with Roasted Beetroot & Rocket

INGREDIENTS

Serves 4

350 g/12 oz raw baby
  beetroot, unpeeled
1 garlic clove, peeled and crushed
½ tsp finely grated orange rind
1 tbsp orange juice
1 tsp lemon juice
2 tbsp walnut oil
salt and freshly ground black pepper
350 g/12 oz dried fettucini
75 g/3 oz rocket leaves
125 g/4 oz Dolcelatte cheese,
  cut into small cubes

HELPFUL HINT

Many large supermarkets sell raw beetroot, but baby beetroot may be more readily available from specialist or ethnic greengrocers. Look for beetroot with the leaves attached. The bulbs should be firm without any soft spots and the leaves should not be wilted.

1 Preheat oven to 150°C/300°F/Gas Mark 2, 10 minutes before cooking. Wrap the beetroot individually in tinfoil and bake for 1–1½ hours, or until tender. Test by opening one of the parcels and scraping the skin away from the stem end – it should come off very easily.

2 Leave the beetroot until cool enough to handle, then peel and cut each beetroot into 6–8 wedges, depending on the size. Mix the garlic, orange rind and juice, lemon juice, walnut oil and salt and pepper together, then drizzle over the beetroot and toss to coat well.

3 Meanwhile, bring a large saucepan of lightly salted water to the boil. Cook the pasta for 10 minutes, or until 'al dente'.

4 Drain the pasta thoroughly, then add the warm beetroot, rocket leaves and Dolcelatte cheese. Quickly and gently toss together, then divide between serving bowls and serve immediately before the rocket wilts.

Pumpkin-filled Pasta with Butter & Sage

INGREDIENTS

Serves 6-8

1 quantity fresh pasta
   dough (see p48)
125 g/4 oz butter
2 tbsp freshly shredded sage leaves
50 g/2 oz freshly grated Parmesan
   cheese, to serve

For the filling:

250 g/9 oz freshly cooked pumpkin
   or sweet potato flesh, mashed
   and cooled
75–125 g/3–4 oz dried breadcrumbs
125 g/4 oz freshly grated
   Parmesan cheese
1 medium egg yolk
½ tsp soft brown sugar
2 tbsp freshly chopped parsley
freshly grated nutmeg
salt and freshly ground black pepper

1 Mix together the ingredients for the filling in a bowl, seasoning to taste with freshly grated nutmeg, salt and pepper. If the mixture seems too wet, add a few more breadcrumbs to bind.

2 Cut the pasta dough (see p48) into quarters. Work with one quarter at a time, covering the remaining quarters with a damp tea towel. Roll out a quarter very thinly into a strip 10 cm/4 inches wide. Drop spoonfuls of the filling along the strip 6.5 cm/2½ inches apart, in 2 rows about 5 cm/2 inches apart. Moisten the outside edges and the spaces between the filling with water.

3 Roll out another strip of pasta and lay it over the filled strip. Press down gently along both edges and between the filled sections. Using a fluted pastry wheel, cut along both long sides, down the centre and between the fillings to form cushions. Transfer the cushions to a lightly floured baking sheet. Continue making cushions and allow to dry for 30 minutes.

4 Bring a large saucepan of slightly salted water to the boil. Add the pasta cushions and return to the boil. Cook, stirring frequently, for 4–5 minutes, or until 'al dente'. Drain carefully.

5 Heat the butter in a pan, stir in the shredded sage leaves and cook for 30 seconds. Add the pasta cushions, stir gently then spoon into serving bowls. Sprinkle with the grated Parmesan cheese and serve immediately.

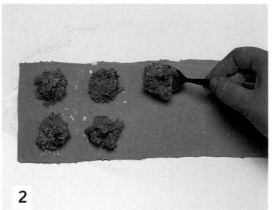

1

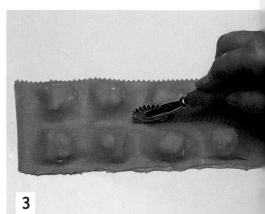

2

3

Pasta with Raw Fennel, Tomato & Red Onions

INGREDIENTS

Serves 6

1 fennel bulb
700 g/1½ lb tomatoes
1 garlic clove
¼ small red onion
small handful fresh basil
small handful fresh mint
100 ml/3½ fl oz extra virgin olive oil,
   plus extra to serve
juice of 1 lemon
salt and freshly ground black pepper
450 g/1 lb penne or pennette
freshly grated Parmesan cheese,
   to serve

1 Trim the fennel and slice thinly. Stack the slices and cut into sticks, then cut crosswise again into fine dice. Deseed the tomatoes and chop them finely. Peel and finely chop or crush the garlic. Peel and finely chop or grate the onion.

2 Stack the basil leaves then roll up tightly. Slice crosswise into fine shreds. Finely chop the mint.

3 Place the chopped vegetables and herbs in a medium bowl. Add the olive oil and lemon juice and mix together. Season well with salt and pepper then leave for 30 minutes to allow the flavours to develop.

4 Bring a large pan of salted water to a rolling boil. Add the pasta and cook according to the packet instructions, or until 'al dente'.

5 Drain the cooked pasta thoroughly. Transfer to a warmed serving dish, pour over the vegetable mixture and toss. Serve with the grated Parmesan cheese and extra olive oil to drizzle over.

HELPFUL HINT

The vegetables used in this dish are not cooked, but are tossed with the hot pasta. It is important, therefore, that they are chopped finely.

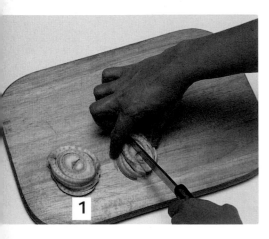

1

2

5

Step-by-Step, Practical Recipes Pasta: Tips & Hints

Food Fact

Garlic is one of the most important flavours in Italian cooking. When buying garlic check it carefully. The heads should be firm without soft spots.

Helpful Hint

Peppers are often used in pasta sauces and sometimes you need to remove their skins. To help do this more easily, first put the peppers in the oven for about 30 minutes or until the skins start to blister. Take them out and put them immediately into a plastic bag or a bowl covered in clingfilm This will cause the peppers to cool more quickly. You will then be able to peel off the skins easily.

Food Fact

A number of fresh herbs are used in Italian cooking, but the most important ones are basil, parsley, rosemary, sage, marjoram and oregano. All are widely available from supermarkets and street markets and, to save money, they can easily be grown in just a small patch of garden or even in a pot on a window sill.

Food Fact

Black olives (see p34) are picked when fully ripe and a brownish pink colour and then fermented and oxidised until they become black. Dry-cured black olives can be bought from Italian food shops or the delicatessen counter of some large supermarkets, but if you are unable to get them, use ordinary small black olives instead.

Helpful Hint

You can still make pesto (see p12) if you do not have a food processor. Tear the basil leaves and place them in a mortar with the garlic, pine nuts and a tablespoonful of the oil. Pound to a paste using a pestle, gradually working in the rest of the oil. Transfer to a bowl and stir in the cheese. Season to taste with salt and pepper. Pesto will keep for 2–3 days if stored in the refrigerator.

Helpful Hint

Chilli flakes (see p14) are made from dried, crushed chillies and are useful for adding heat to pasta dishes that are meant to be quite spicy. There are lots of other chilli products that you could use as well. For instance, a tablespoonful of chilli oil for one of the tablespoons of olive oil or simply add a dash of tabasco sauce at the end of cooking.

Helpful Hint

Never clean mushrooms (see p24) under running water. Mushrooms absorb any liquid easily and then release it again during cooking, making the dish watery. When cleaning mushrooms, especially if they are from a market or are wild, wipe them with a damp cloth or use a soft brush to remove grit. Cut off the bases and the stems to remove further dirt.

Food Fact

Rocket (see p42) was first introduced to Europe in the late 16th century, but went out of fashion during Victorian times.

The tender tiny leaves have the most delicate flavour and, as they grow in size, their peppery flavour becomes much more pronounced.

Tasty Tip

For a rich tomato sauce, which is central to many pasta dishes, roughly chop 900 g/2 lb ripe tomatoes, then place in a saucepan with 1 crushed garlic clove, 1 tablespoon olive oil and 2 tablespoons Worcestershire sauce. Cook until soft, then sieve or purèe. You can refrigerate or freeze any leftover sauce and then reheat it later and serve with a new batch of freshly cooked pasta.

Helpful Hint

Fresh pasta takes much less time to cook than dried pasta and 2–3 minutes is usually long enough for it to be 'al dente'. Tagliatelle comes from Bologna, where it is usually served with a meat sauce. Green tagliatelle is generally flavoured with spinach, but it is also available flavoured with fresh herbs, which would go particularly well with the rich cheese sauces found in many pasta recipes.

Food Fact

Home-made pasta has a light, almost silky texture and is very different from bought fresh pasta. The pasta dough (see p6 and 44) is made from pasta flour, salt, eggs, olive oil and water. The dough is then rolled out and cut into strips. A pasta maker can be useful if you make this pasta regularly.

First published in 2012 by
FLAME TREE PUBLISHING LTD
Crabtree Hall, Crabtree Lane, Fulham,
London, SW6 6TY, United Kingdom
www.flametreepublishing.com

NOTE: Recipes using uncooked eggs should be avoided by infants, the elderly, pregnant women and anyone suffering from an illness.

18 17 16 15 14 13 12   10 9 8 7 6 5 4 3 2 1

ISBN: 978-0-85775-607-7

ACKNOWLEDGEMENTS: Authors: Catherine Atkinson, Juliet Barker, Gina Steer, Vicki Smallwood, Carol Tennant, Mari Mererid Williams, Elizabeth Wolf-Cohen and Simone Wright. Photography: Colin Bowling, Paul Forrester and Stephen Brayne. Home Economists and Stylists: Jacqueline Bellefontaine, Mandy Phipps, Vicki Smallwood and Penny Stephens. All props supplied by Barbara Stewart at Surfaces. Publisher and Creative Director: Nick Wells. Editorial: Catherine Taylor, Sarah Goulding, Marcus Hardie, Gina Steer and Karen Fitzpatrick. Design and Production: Chris Herbert, Mike Spender, Colin Rudderham and Helen Wall.